What's Going on When It's

by Noah Leatherland

Minneapolis, Minnesota

Credits

Images are courtesy of Shutterstock.com. With thanks to Getty Images, Thinkstock Photo, and iStockphoto. Cover – MeSamong, rogger design, Gaidamashchuk, AlexanderTrou. Texture throughout – MeSamong. 4–5 – Skreidzeleu, Brian A Jackson, nataka, Robert Latham, travnikovstudio. 6–7 – aleks333, Jacob_09. 8–9 – solarseven, Subbotina Anna, Yellow duck. 10–11 – Lizavetta, BlueRingMedia. 12–13 – Pablesku, Patrick Foto, Guppic the duck. 14–15 – Crazy Owl Productions, Lamyai, quielines. 16–17 – Piyaset, denayunebgt, J.J. Gouin. 18–19 – Toa55, Alaskagirl8821, sotisare. 20–21 – Nancy Hixson, atsurkan. 22–23 – PeopleImages.com - Yuri A, verona studio, Karelkart.

Bearport Publishing Company Product Development Team

Publisher: Jen Jenson; Director of Product Development: Spencer Brinker; Managing Editor: Allison Juda; Editor: Cole Nelson; Associate Editor: Naomi Reich; Associate Editor: Tiana Tran; Art Director: Colin O'Dea; Designer: Kim Jones; Designer: Kayla Eggert; Product Development Specialist: Owen Hamlin

Library of Congress Cataloging-in-Publication Data is available at www.loc.gov or upon request from the publisher.

ISBN: 979-8-89232-871-5 (hardcover)
ISBN: 979-8-89232-957-6 (paperback)
ISBN: 979-8-89232-901-9 (ebook)

For more information, write to Bearport Publishing, 5357 Penn Avenue South, Minneapolis, MN 55419.

CONTENTS

WHAT IS WEATHER?

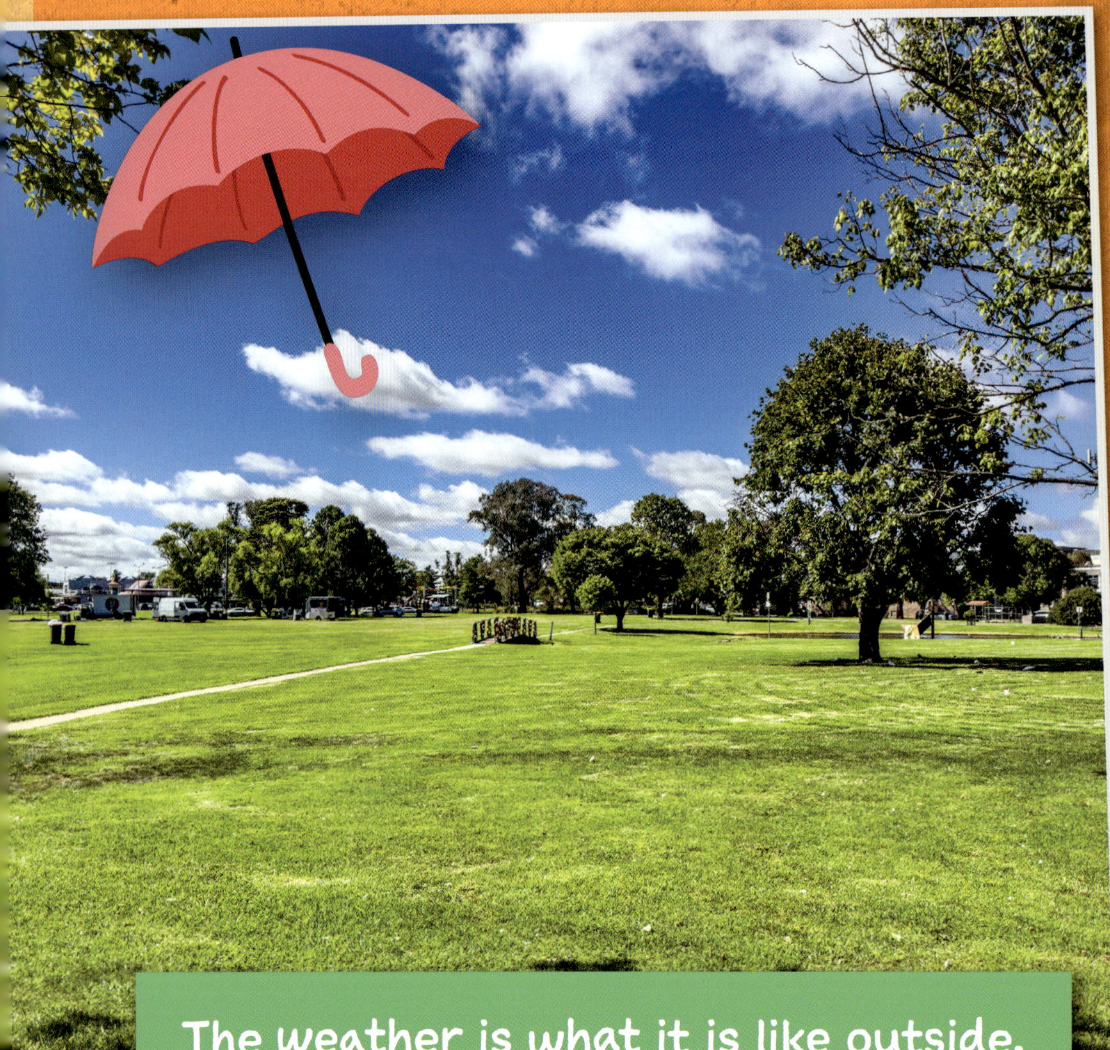

The weather is what it is like outside. Weather is always changing.

Many things can affect the weather. Heat waves make it very hot outside. Summer can bring sunny, warm days.

WHAT'S GOING ON WHEN IT GETS HOT?

TEMPERATURE

Temperature is how hot or cold something is. It is one way to measure the weather.

Some places are hot or cold all year. Other places change temperatures each season.

SUNSHINE

The sun gives heat and light to Earth. The sun's heat is what makes life possible here.

Some days have more sun than others. Often, clouds can block the sun. The sun shines more in some seasons than in others.

WARM

SUMMERS

Summer is the hottest season of the year. The days are longer, which usually means there is more sunshine.

Earth has seasons because it is **tilted** as it circles the sun. Summer happens on the side tilted toward the sun.

HELPFUL HEAT

Warm weather is helpful to plants. Plants need sunshine to make food. This is easier for them to do in warm weather.

Sunshine also helps humans. It can help our bodies make the **vitamins** we need. But too much sun can hurt our skin.

HEAT WAVES

A heat wave happens when the weather gets much hotter than usual. Heat waves can last a few days or even months.

People can get hot very quickly during a heat wave. They can get hurt if they can't cool down.

DROUGHTS

Hot weather often means less rain. This can make a **drought.** A drought happens when there is not enough water.

It is harder for plants to grow during droughts. Farmers may struggle to grow **crops**.

WILDFIRES

Hot weather can make trees and other plants very dry. Dry trees can catch fire very easily. This can start a wildfire.

Wildfires can spread very quickly and cause a lot of damage. They can hurt animals and people living close by.

STAYING
HYDRATED

Hot weather can make you sweat. Sweat cools your body as it dries. This can keep you from getting too hot.

Your body loses water through sweat. It is important to drink more water to stay **hydrated** in hot weather.

HOT
DAYS

Hot weather can be great for swimming or playing outside. But be careful! Too much sun can burn your skin.

Sunscreen helps block sunlight. It can keep your skin safe while you have fun outdoors!

GLOSSARY

crops plants that are grown to be eaten

drought a long period of dry weather

hydrated to have drunk enough water for the body to work

sunscreen a lotion placed on the skin to protect it from sun damage

tilted leaning to one side

vitamins substances needed for normal and healthy growth

INDEX